The ARTS

MUSIC

Alan Blackwood

STECK-VAUGHN
LIBRARY
Austin·Texas

The Arts

Architecture
Dance
Design
Literature
The Movies

Music
Painting and Sculpture
Photography
Theater

Cover illustration: Young musicians on trumpet and accordion entertaining passersby in a city square.

Series and Book Editor: Rosemary Ashley
Designer: David Armitage
Consultant: Percy Young, MA, MUS.D, D.MUS
Musical advisor and one-time Director of Musical Education.

Published in the United States in 1990 by Steck-Vaughn Co., Austin, Texas, a subsidiary of National Education Corporation.

First published in 1988 by
Wayland (Publishers) Limited

Library of Congress Cataloging-in-Publication Data

Blackwood, Alan, 1932–
    Music / Alan Blackwood.
       p.   cm.—(The Arts)
    "First published in 1988 by Wayland (Publishers) Limited"—T.p. verso.
    Bibliography: p.
    Includes index.
    Summary: Surveys music throughout the ages, including musical instruments, the development of classical music, jazz, folk music, Eastern music, opera, pop music, and the mechanics of broadcasting and recording.

    ISBN 0–8114–2358–1
    1. Music—History and criticism—Juvenile literature.
    I. Title.   II. Series: Arts (Austin, Tex.)
ML3929.852   1989
780—dc20
                                                    89–11479
                                                       CIP
                                                     AC MN

Typeset by DP Press, Sevenoaks, England
Printed in Italy
Bound in the United States

1 2 3 4 5 6 7 8 9 0 SA 95 94 93 92 91 90

Contents

1 What is Music ?

It is not easy to define music: one way might be to describe it as organized sound. However, this does not explain its special effects on all of us. We cannot see music, or touch it; yet it can make us feel happy or sad or excite us, more quickly than any images or words. Much of music's special magic comes from the fact that it is a shared experience among many people. It is an art that people make together: musicians create music and audiences listen. Because of this sharing element, music is the most popular of all the arts and holds the greatest attraction for people all over the world.

People of many civilizations have regarded music as a gift from the gods. The ancient Greeks spoke of Mount Parnassus as the sacred home of the muses – the spirits who inspired men and women to play and sing beautiful music. This is where the word music comes from. In fact, the Greeks believed the whole universe – earth, sun, moon and stars – was ruled by marvelous harmonies.

Below *A Roman mural at Herculaneum, near Pompeii in Italy, showing a young woman learning to play the kithara, a type of lyre. Although we know a good deal about ancient Greek and Roman musical instruments, we have only a vague idea of how music was played and sung in ancient times.*

It was this belief in a heavenly "Music of the Spheres" that prompted the Greek philosopher Pythagoras to investigate some of the facts about musical sounds. He found that the length of a vibrating cord or string is directly related to the pitch (the highness or lowness) of the sound it makes. As the length of the cord is shortened, so it vibrates faster, and produces sounds that go up in pitch. He then worked out, in simple mathematics, the relationships between different lengths of cord and sounds of different pitch. We can achieve the same effect by tightening a cord or elastic band. As it is pulled tighter it will vibrate faster when plucked, and the pitch will be higher.

Pythagoras was a pioneer in the science of acoustics – the study of sound, especially musical sounds. All sounds are created when something vibrates. These vibrations cause what are called sound waves in the surrounding air (or water); though it is better to think of them as a kind of throbbing or pulsation of the air . When these waves or pulsations reach our ears, they make our eardrums vibrate at the same rate, and so we hear the sounds. The speed or rapidity of sound waves is called their frequency. The higher (or faster) the frequency, the higher will be the pitch of a note, just as Pythagoras discovered.

But musical sounds are not just a matter of pitch. Almost equally important is their tone. This is the quality of their sound; the quality that makes, for example, the sound of a violin and a trumpet quite different, even when they are playing a note of exactly the same pitch. Nearly all musical sounds consist of many different vibrations. The vibration that produces the pitch of the note as we hear it is called the fundamental. Then there are other vibrations within it that produce more sounds of rising pitch, called overtones. It is the way these overtones blend that gives a sound its own special tone. It is sometimes quite easy to hear this in the tolling of a bell.

5

The elements of music

Musicians use the elements of melody, harmony, and rhythm, which they put together in different ways to create music.

Melody is a simple progression or line of musical sounds or notes, rising or falling in pitch. A simple melody may have only three or four notes, while a more complex one may go on for thirty or forty notes. Nearly all melodies have an underlying scale structure. Scales are a sequence of notes arranged in order, going up or down in pitch. One of the oldest types of scale is the pentatonic – meaning five notes – still the basis of much Eastern music and common in the folk music of many European countries. But the scales most familiar to us have eight notes each. There are major scales, in which the notes are arranged in one particular sequence of pitches; these have a bright sound. Minor scales follow a different arrangement and have a dramatic sound. Composers select the notes from a scale to create a melody. Major and/or minor scales can be built upon any tone.

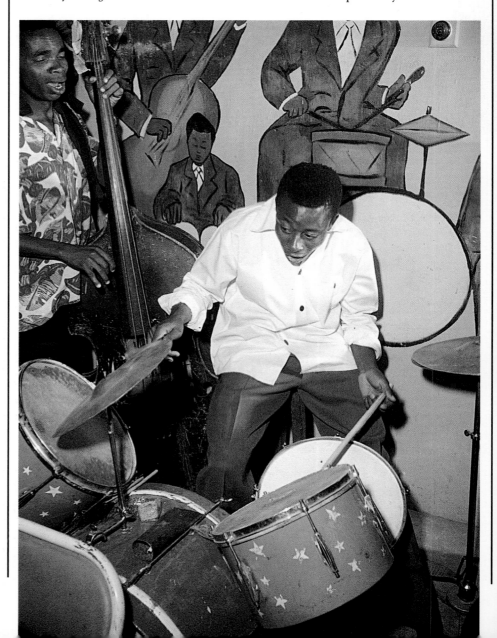

A jazz drummer in New Orleans. Drums are the main instruments of rhythm, and the strong rhythmic beat of much jazz, especially of the kind originating in New Orleans, is one of its biggest attractions.

Many melodies can sound beautiful or exciting on their own. But we usually hear them played or sung with added harmonies. Harmony is the sounding of two or more notes of different pitch. We often say that harmonies "support" a melody, as though they were the struts or arches of a bridge. They can also give a melody a special mood or character.

Rhythm paces or measures out a melody. The rhythms most familiar to us are based on a steady beat, almost as regular as the tick of a clock. The notes of the tune or melody then fit into this beat or tempo, some notes usually being of longer or shorter duration than others, just as they are of different pitch. And just as harmonies can change the mood or feeling of a melody, so fitting a melody to a different rhythm can also change it. In fact, rhythm is so important that we can often enjoy it on its own – for example, in the beat of a drum – while most melodies without rhythm seem somewhat shapeless and uninteresting.

The way a piece of music is put together is called its form. A tune or melody has its own form, often consisting of an opening phrase, or group of notes, then a different middle phrase, followed by a repeat of the opening phrase. Many melodies are a part of some larger musical composition, which has a form of its own, just as the form of a whole painting is made up of many parts. An important aspect of musical form is the way phrases of melody and rhythm are repeated many times over, forming regular patterns of sound.

Above *The Dutch conductor Bernard Haitinck, directing the London Philharmonic Orchestra. A modern symphony orchestra may contain more than a hundred players. Symphony orchestras perform mainly in the countries of North America, Europe, and the Soviet Union, where there is a long tradition of playing orchestral music.*

2 Musical Instruments

Thousands of years ago, people made musical instruments from natural objects around them, such as shells and stones, or animal skins and bones. They may have played these to summon up the spirits of the dead, or to communicate with their gods.

Since those ancient times, musical instruments have been made in an astonishing variety of shapes, sizes, and materials, all of which help to give them their own special sound. One way of classifying instruments is according to their source of sound. *Chordophones* (stringed instruments) have vibrating strings; and *membranophones* (drums) have a vibrating skin or similar material. Such instruments also need a resonator, a framework that takes up the vibrations and makes them sound stronger and richer. *Idiophones* (percussion instruments other than drums) do not need a resonator, as their whole substance vibrates as one. *Aerophones* (wind instruments) have tubes or pipes that produce and amplify vibrating columns of air.

Below *The violinist draws her bow across the strings of her instruments to make them vibrate, while she "stops" or adjusts their playing length with her fingers, to produce notes of different pitch.*

Below *A street musician in Nepal plays a handmade stringed instrument. Its most striking feature is the large, bulbous resonator, which picks up the vibrations of the strings and gives them a richer tone.*

Illustrated are instruments of the violin family. Increasing in size, with longer, thicker strings, each sounds a range of notes of lower pitch. All have four strings played with a bow, or plucked (pizzicato).

Strings

Apart from the harp, which has a string for each note that it sounds, most stringed instruments have only a few strings. These can be pressed down by the player's fingers so that they vibrate for only a part of their length, to sound notes of different pitch. This is called "stopping" the strings. The thickness and tightness of the strings also affects the pitch of the notes, since thin or tight strings vibrate faster than thick or loose ones.

The main division among stringed instruments is between those on which the player plucks the strings – harps, lutes, guitars, sitars – and those on which the strings are vibrated with a bow. An early type of bowed stringed instrument was the Arabic rebec. Today, the violin, viola, cello, and double bass are the most important bowed stringed instruments (although their strings can be plucked also). Each is progressively larger in size, and with longer, thicker strings, which means that each, in turn, sounds a range of notes deeper in pitch.

Above *An Indian instrument maker displaying and demonstrating his wares. Wooden pipes like these are among the commonest forms of wind instruments around the world.*

The principal woodwind instruments. Flutes produce the highest pitched tones; oboes are deeper; clarinets sound slightly deeper, sharpening on high notes; bassoons are like oboes but bigger. (Not drawn to scale)

The resonance of stringed instruments, and especially of the violin family, is very important. Their wooden frames give richness and depth of tone to the vibrating strings, which on their own make a very thin sound.

Woodwind and brass

With wind instruments the player uses his breath to make the air vibrate inside them. The length and diameter (bore) of the tube or pipe, and the type of mouthpiece attached, all affect the volume, pitch, and tone of the notes they sound. Indeed, the size of wind instruments varies enormously, from the smallest whistle pipe to the gigantic Alpine and Tibetan horns whose sound can carry over great distances. However, the main difference is between woodwind and brass.

Panpipes are a type of woodwind instrument, with a pipe of different size for each pitched note. But panpipes are not typical of woodwind instruments as a whole. At one time these were nearly all made from wood. But the name now describes the way they are played rather than the material they are made from, which is often metal.

The saxophone is a cross between a woodwind and a brass instrument. It was originally intended for military bands but has become a favorite jazz instrument. Sizes range from the small, high-pitched soprano, to the much larger, deeper-sounding baritone and bass.

11

Flutes and recorders have a mouthpiece that directs the player's breath into the pipe. The various types of clarinet, oboe, and bassoon have a mouthpiece fitted with a thin reed (or reeds), which the player vibrates with his or her breath.

Woodwind instruments also have holes in their tube or pipe. By closing or opening these, the player changes the rate of vibrations and so produces notes of different pitch (a little like a violinist "stopping" the strings).

Brass instruments are made from metal; but again it is their design and method of playing that really distinguishes them. The basic method of playing them can be seen in such ancient instruments as the Jewish shofar, made from a ram's horn, or the conch seashell. With these the player presses the lips against one end and blows hard. This produces sound waves inside the horn or shell. True brass instruments have a small cup-shaped mouthpiece, into which the player blows and vibrates the lips. The tube itself is another feature of brass instruments. It has a conical bore (one that gradually widens), opening right out into what is called its bell.

For centuries brass instruments were made of one long tube, straight or coiled. Because of this, they could only sound three or four notes with any reliability – their fundamental and basic overtones, as described on page 5. But modern trumpets and horns, and the deeper-pitched tuba, have piston valves that change the overall length of the tube, so that the player can sound many more notes. The trombone has a sliding valve that alters the length of the tube.

Below *Today's four most important brass instruments. They can sound brilliant and brazen, or haunting when played quietly. The tuba is used to produce a deep sound that underlies the other instruments of the orchestra. (Not drawn to scale)*

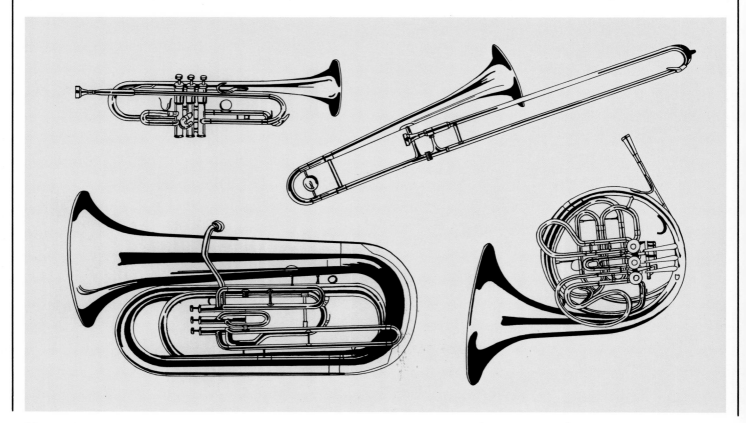

An oddity among wind instruments is the bagpipe, in its many shapes and sizes. It has a bag or sack into which the piper blows a reservoir of air. This leads to one or more pipes that can play a tune (chanters) or sound a single note (drone).

Another wind instrument in a class of its own is the saxophone, named after its Belgian inventor Adolphe Sax. It has a conical tube with a bell, like a brass instrument, but also holes in the tube and a reed mouthpiece, like a woodwind. Saxophones are made in various sizes, each with a different range of pitched notes.

Percussion

Percussion instruments are all those that are struck to make them vibrate, hence they are mainly instruments of rhythm rather than of melody. Most important are drums, with their skin or other material stretched over an enclosed frame, which is their resonator.

Most other percussion instruments are *idiophones* (which do not need a resonator). There is a great range of them: xylophones and marimbas (which can play tunes because they have a different-sized block of wood or metal for each note); gongs and cymbals; bells, from tinkling hand bells to giant ones weighing many tons; triangles, wood blocks, clappers, castanets, rattles, even stones.

One other important division among percussion instruments is between those of definite pitch (those that sound a particular note, like kettledrums, xylophones, bells); and those of indefinite pitch (those whose note is difficult or impossible to sing to, such as gongs, cymbals, and other kinds of drums).

Above *A percussion band at carnival time in Rio de Janeiro, Brazil. Some percussion instruments, such as cymbals, and the tambourines and maracas of this band, can only sound one note. Other percussion instruments, such as kettledrums, steel drums, and xylophones sound notes of different pitch and can therefore play tunes.*

Keyboard and mechanical instruments

Another class of instruments are those with a row of keys which the player presses down to sound the notes.

Stringed keyboard instruments have a set of strings of different length, much like those of a harp. Their wooden frame acts as a resonator. In the case of early instruments of this type, the virginals, spinet, and harpsichord, the keys operate small devices called jacks, that pluck the strings. The more recent piano, by contrast, has hammers that strike the strings instead of plucking them. By varying their finger pressure, and using the pedals, pianists can widen the range of their instrument to sound far softer or sustain the notes far longer than a harpsichord. The full name for the piano is pianoforte – "soft-loud" in Italian.

The keyboard of the organ operates a mechanism that admits air into a range of pipes, each sounding its own note. This "King of Instruments" has a colorful history. The Romans made a kind of organ (the hydraulus) that used water pressure to supply air to the pipes. Medieval organs had wooden "sliders" instead of a keyboard, that the player had to push in and out to admit air to the pipes, while others worked a huge set of bellows. There were also very small models that people could carry with them. Large modern organs have hundreds of pipes, several keyboards, including a pedal board that the organist plays with his feet, and draw-stops that make one set of pipes sound instead of another.

Keyboards have been applied to other instruments, such as the celesta, in which they strike small metal bars; and the accordion which is a modern type of portable organ.

Before the days of recording (see page 43), some pianos and organs were designed to play mechanically. Sheets of perforated paper controlled a supply of air that worked the keyboard and played pieces of music. In days gone by, there were many other mechanical instruments, including musical boxes with revolving cylinders that struck a row of small metal teeth.

Left *Ella Fitzgerald (1918–) has been a leading solo jazz singer for more than forty years. She performs popular songs in an individual style, often making up sounds instead of singing words. Such "scat" singing demonstrates the marvelous versatility of the human voice.*

Below *Some traditional instruments, such as the acoustic (Spanish) guitar, have been fitted with electrical apparatus, which has changed the quality or tone of their sounds. Electric guitars have metal strings and their sound is produced by an amplifier and loudspeaker.*

The voice

This is our very own musical instrument and it operates much like other instruments. The sources of sound of the voice are the small vocal cords in the front part of the throat, called the larynx. When we tighten them, we can make them vibrate, using breath from our lungs. The tighter we stretch them, the faster they vibrate, producing higher-pitched sounds. Our palate, tongue, and teeth all help to shape the sounds from the larynx. The rest of the head, throat, and torso all act as resonators, giving power and character to the voice.

The sound of men's and women's voices differs, mainly because of the size and toughness of the vocal cords. A boy's voice is said to change when these start to toughen up. (The vocal cords harden in girls too, but not to the same extent.) Men's voices range in pitch from deep down in the bass, up through baritone, to tenor and high-pitched counter-tenor. Women's voices range from the fairly low-pitched contralto to high soprano.

Because our voices are a part of us, we can do more with them than with any other instrument, and we can combine words with melody. No other instrument can do that.

Electric and electronic instruments

All the instruments we have looked at so far have existed, in one form or another, for hundreds, even thousands of years. But in this century we have seen a musical revolution.

The basis of this revolution is the connection between sound waves and radio waves, and how one can be converted into the other. Some inventors have adapted existing instruments for this purpose. Such instruments are still played in the usual way, but they operate

electrical devices that actually produce the sounds. The electric guitar still has strings, but when these vibrate they activate electrical impulses which are turned back into sound and amplified by a loudspeaker. The sounds are quite different from those of the traditional Spanish or acoustic guitar. Electric organs have a keyboard, but they also operate electronic devices, so there is no need of pipes. A more original instrument with a keyboard is the ondes Martenot. Its electrical oscillations or waves are amplified to produce a strange, otherworldly tone that has inspired music from several composers.

Tape recorders have also interested composers. By recording sounds, playing them back faster or slower, or cutting them up and re-assembling them in a different order, and then re-recording the results, composers have turned the most commonplace noises into amazing sequences or patterns of sound.

A real breakthrough into a whole new world of sound came with the synthesizer. The name means "to build up." A synthesizer does exactly this, by electronically producing all kinds of basic wave patterns, mixing them together and turning them into sounds, much as the colors of the spectrum might be split up and then re-combined to produce new shades and intensities of light. Indeed, people who work with synthesizers speak of such things as "white sound," or "square waves" and "filters," suggesting a fascinating link between sounds, colors, and shapes. Today "sequencers" and computers are programmed to work out and memorize millions of sound and radio patterns for synthesizers to use.

Above *Electronic instruments have given music a new dimension, producing sounds in ways that are completely different from more traditional instruments. The first synthesizers were made in the 1960s by the American inventor Robert Moog. Today's models can produce and combine every conceivable kind of sound by electronic means and are used by pop musicians, and by such modern composers as Karlheinz Stockhausen (1928–).*

③ Music Around The World

All over the world, in every land, people make music. Their melodies, harmonies, and rhythms may differ, but their instruments are made to the same basic principles, and they express through their music many of the same thoughts and feelings. Some of the music can be called "classical," in the sense that it is serious, as opposed to "popular" music. Much of it is folk music – music created by peoples or cultures often going back thousands of years. Much folk music probably began as a recitation of even older myths and legends, or as songs and dances with some magical and ritual purpose. What has come down to us, from generation to generation, as a colorful and quaint old folk song or dance, may at one time have had a quite different, even grim meaning.

Eastern music

The countries of India, China, Japan, and Indonesia each possess their own kind of music. But all Eastern music has a basic similarity – the music is played or sung so that single lines of musical sounds, or notes, follow one another to create melodies.

The traditional music of India is the raga. Its form has been handed down for generations; but within that form, the small group of musicians (including sometimes a singer) improvise – display their

Indian musicians performing a raga. The basic form or style of ragas has changed very little in a thousand years; but the players make subtle improvisations (changes in melody and harmony) as they play, so that every performance is unique.

skills at making up music on the spur of the moment. The raga itself is a type of scale, which serves as the basis for a particular performance. The leading player, usually on the sitar, plays it at the start; then all the players begin to play quietly and thoughtfully, feeling their way into the mood of the raga, before settling into a steady rhythm with an unfolding melody. The pace quickens, and the music reaches a climax. Different ragas are associated with certain seasons of the year, or times of day, and may only be played on those occasions.

The old empires of China and Japan were noted for their elaborate court ceremonies. These are reflected in forms of stage play with music, in which every word and sound, even the slightest movement, is significant. Chinese instruments that accompany the singing and dancing include the piba (a type of lute), the sheng (a cross between the panpipes and bagpipes), drums, and clappers. The musicians also play delicate pieces evoking scenes from nature. Japanese musicians play the koto (a type of zither), shamisu (another type of lute), and shakuhachi (bamboo flute). Both Chinese and Japanese music use pentatonic scales but the notes are not the same, so that the character of each type of traditional music is quite different.

The tropical islands of Indonesia are famous for their gamelan bands. The instruments are nearly all percussion, such as the bonang (chiming gongs) and gambang (xylophone). Many of them also sound pitched notes, tuned to another type of pentatonic scale. Gamelan rhythms and melodies often sound hypnotic.

Right *A drum and pipe band in Bolivia. The pipes are a kind of panpipe, with a pipe of different length for each pitched note. Such traditional instruments are found in many parts of the world.*

Inset right *A large gamelan band in session. In Indonesia, many villages make their own instruments, so that every band has its own special and uniquely beautiful sound. Gamelans play for all kinds of occasions – weddings, social gatherings, religious ceremonies, and theatrical performances.*

Below *A Caribbean steel band playing on the sands of the Bahamas. The band contains instruments called pans, originally made from oil drums. When struck, they produce notes with a ringing sound.*

Native Australian music

One of the oldest cultures in the world is that of the Australian Aborigines, probably remaining unchanged for thousands of years, until the arrival of Europeans two centuries ago. What is left of their age-old way of life, including their music, is therefore of great interest. The Aborigines have instruments of a kind rarely found anywhere else. The didgeridoo is a hollowed-out part of a tree. The player blows

into it in a way similar to a brass instrument; but he uses his own voice to add to its sound and manages also to keep blowing and breathing at the same time, thus maintaining a continuous drone-like sound. Another almost unique device, not belonging to any known category of instrument, is the thunder stick or bull roarer, a flat piece of wood on a length of rope, rotated in the air to make a whirring sound. The chanting and hand-clapping that go with these primitive instruments can set up very complex rhythms.

Music in the Americas

It is probable that thousands of years ago, the people we now know as native American Indians crossed the Bering Strait from Asia to Alaska and migrated south. Some of the instruments they still use, such as the Amazonian wood pipes, and the American Indians' thunder stick, are similar to those of the Aborigines, showing how people living entirely apart discovered much the same ways of producing musical sounds. Much of the actual singing and dancing of pre-Columbian America (before the arrival of Columbus) has been preserved although may be influenced somewhat by more recent music.

American music is a rich blend of styles. It comes partly from the Spanish and Portuguese, who colonized nearly all of South and Central America (Latin America); and partly from the sad history of the black people of the Caribbean and southeastern United States, who were originally shipped from Africa as slaves. This mixture of traditions, including those coming from Europe, has given us music of many different styles. They include spirituals, blues, and popular Latin American dance music such as the rhumba and samba; also the Caribbean steel bands, and calypso and reggae songs. Such music has had a tremendous influence on the world of popular music, which we discuss later on.

African music

Continuing around the world, the true music of Africa belongs to the black races who live south of the Sahara. From prehistoric times, music has been for them something as vital as breathing and eating. They have created instruments of nearly all the types we have so far discussed, using some of them in unusual ways. The player may use a bow on his one-stringed fiddle, while also gripping the string between his teeth, using his mouth to give the sounds resonance and tone. Giant xylophones are sometimes placed over holes in the ground – again to give them added resonance – which several people can play at once. Above all, there are the drums. One is the hour-glass drum, which can be compressed, thus changing its shape and the pitch of its sound. Drums have been of prime importance throughout black Africa, as a way of sending messages. Songs have also been used as a means of communication, and are still used as a way of communicating protest.

Above *A Spanish flamenco dancer performing to the music of an acoustic guitar. The acoustic guitar has six strings and is capable of a great range of music, from concertos to solo pieces and accompaniment for singers. It is traditionally used for flamenco music in Spain.*

Inset left *A member of a brass band playing a large horn called a sousaphone, in a fiesta procession in South America. The horn was named after the American bandmaster and composer John Phillip Sousa (1854–1932).*

Left *Young drummers in a Kenyan village beating out rhythms on their drums. They demonstrate the importance of drums in much African music.*

European folk music

The music of large parts of Europe has links with the Islamic civilization. Muslim armies first swept across North Africa and in the eighth century on into Spain. At a later date, the Islamic Turkish, or Ottoman, Empire spread over much of Eastern Europe. In Greece and Yugoslavia, we can hear and see evidence of the Islamic world in their folk music, dance, and musical instruments.

The most striking legacy of all this Islamic influence is the singing and dancing of Spanish flamenco. Its homeland is the province of Andalusia in southern Spain. Part of flamenco is called *cante hondo*, meaning "deep song," in which the singer chants melodies, with many repetitions of one note, that have a strong Moorish (North African) sound. There is also energetic and passionate dancing, accompanied by the strum of guitars and the click of handheld castanets.

In parts of Britain, and France, some of the ancient ways of the Celtic people have survived, especially in song and dance. The Irish clàrsach, a small harp, and the Welsh crwth, a type of stringed lyre played with a bow, may date from those ancient times. Scotland is a part of old Celtic Britain, famous for its special type of bagpipe music. Its reels and other lively dances may have come originally from Scandinavia.

Early British settlers in North America enjoyed dancing reels. Reels, in turn, led to some of the old American hillbilly songs and square dances, often performed to fiddle or accordion accompaniment. These are still very much alive today in the popular music known as country and western. In such ways music spreads and changes all the time.

4 Western Music

Western music means the music of the whole of Europe, and of those other countries with strong European connections. It is also the music that people often call "classical." Over the last thousand years, this music has grown and changed more rapidly than that of any other civilization, largely because of its notation — its system of writing music down. This has provided for an accumulating store of musical knowledge, and encouraged composers to keep building upon it. It has also allowed them to create new music with as much thought and care as authors write books and plays. Today we think of it as music for serious listening; but it did not start that way.

The Middle Ages
The first important Western or European music was church music, called plainsong, or plainchant. This consisted of simple, slow-moving melodies, sung by a choir. They were based partly on old

Below *Instruments of the type depicted in this fourteenth-century illustration were popular among the troubadours and other minstrels of the Middle Ages.*

Hebrew chants of biblical times, and partly on scales called modes, that had a connection with Greek music. Plainsong is still sung to the traditional words of some church services, and the best-known form is the Gregorian Chant, named after Pope Gregory I (c. AD 540–604).

Plainsong at first had no harmonies. But gradually, musicians added harmony as they found out how to combine melodies. This was the start of polyphony (notes of more than one melody sounding together). To help choirs learn this more complicated music, musicians invented a form of notation. By the early thirteenth century they were using the basic system of writing music that we use today.

Not all medieval music was religious. Minstrels entertained people with their songs, often accompanying themselves on a harp. Some of the best-known of these minstrels were noblemen, even including royalty – King Richard I of England was a notable minstrel. Those living in southern France were called troubadours, and in Germany there were "minnesingers" or singers of love. All these minstrels enjoyed contests of singing and poetry. The Celtic bards or minstrels of Wales called their contests eisteddfodau (sessions or gatherings). Today's Welsh eisteddfods continue this tradition.

Below *A sixteenth-century painting by an unknown Italian artist of musicians performing a concert in the countryside. They are playing the viol, recorder, lute, and virginals.*

Renaissance music

The Renaissance of the fifteenth and sixteenth centuries brought about a rapid development in music. The polyphony we have talked about grew richer in sound. One piece of church music, by the English composer Thomas Tallis, has forty different melodic lines or parts, all sounding together.

The powerful and wealthy monarchs and noble families of the Renaissance demanded music for entertainment; and many composers wrote secular (nonreligious) pieces for them, such as madrigals (songs for four or five singers only) and dances. Monteverdi wrote madrigals for the rich Gonzaga family in Italy, and in England Thomas Morley and John Dowland wrote and performed songs with lute accompaniment for the nobility.

The Renaissance was also a time of new industrial skills, and saw the manufacture of new or improved musical instruments; trumpets, horns, and trombones; bowed stringed instruments called viols; and keyboard instruments, including organs and the new stringed virginals and harpsichords. Wealthy people were eager to buy these, and composers to write pieces for them. William Byrd and Orlando

Above *George Frederick Handel (1685–1759) wrote his* Music for the Royal Fireworks *for a grand firework display in London to celebrate a peace treaty in 1749. Handel spent most of his life in London, writing operas and oratorios in the Baroque style.*

Gibbons in England, and Antonio de Cabezón in Spain, wrote some of the first important keyboard music. Giovanni Gabrieli, in Venice, composed some splendid music for brass instruments. At this same time, music began to be published.

These advances in music, together with the improved ability of musicians, spurred the imagination of composers, who began to produce works of greater musical structure.

Baroque music

The period following the Renaissance, from about 1600 to 1750, was known as the Baroque period, and Baroque music was in the same mood or style as the grand architecture and opulent paintings of the time. This period saw the growth of opera, the grandest of all art forms (which we look at more closely on pages 32–36), and of oratorio, which usually included a choir, soloists, and instruments.

Above *Ludwig van Beethoven (1770– 1827) was a new and revolutionary kind of artist who insisted on his artistic independence. He began to go deaf in his twenties and had lost his hearing completely by 1824. Despite this handicap he continued to compose music of great dramatic power.*

Above *Johann Sebastian Bach (1685– 1750) seated at the keyboard, with his large family around him. Two of his sons, Carl Philipp Emanuel and Johann Christian, became famous composers in their turn.*

Some Famous Concertos	
Bach	*Brandenburg Concertos*
	Double Violin Concerto
Haydn	*Trumpet Concerto*
Mozart	*Piano Concerto no 26 (Coronation)*
	Clarinet Concerto
Beethoven	*Piano Concerto no 5 (Emperor)*
Mendelssohn	*Violin Concerto in E minor*
Brahms	*Violin Concerto in D major*
Grieg	*Piano Concerto in A minor*
Tchaikovsky	*Piano Concerto no 1*
Rachmaninov	*Piano Concerto no 2*
Sibelius	*Violin Concerto in D minor*
Elgar	*Cello Concerto in E minor*
Rodrigo	*Guitar Concerto (Concierto de Aranjuez)*

Baroque music also continued the Renaissance interest in instruments. Craftsmen, such as Niccolo Amati and Antonio Stradivari, made violins, which sounded a sharper, clearer note than viols, and could also be played with greater agility. These, and the deeper-toned violas and cellos, inspired Corelli, Vivaldi, and many other composers to write new forms of instrumental music. One of these was the concerto, meaning "playing together," because such pieces were written for a group of mostly stringed instruments. There were also sonatas (meaning to sound) for three or four instruments. Beautifully made organs and harpsichords prompted Scarlatti, Couperin, and others to write new kinds of keyboard music; sets of dances called suites, and intricately worked out pieces called fugues.

Most Baroque musical forms and styles began in Italy; but the two greatest composers of the period were both German. J.S. Bach was an organist and choirmaster who wrote music of wonderful variety — great choral works and cantatas, fugues, and other contrapuntal pieces (in which parts of melodies are intricately interwoven) for organ and harpsichord, orchestral concertos, and sets of lively suites. The other great composer of the time was Handel. He was born in Germany but lived in London, where he composed many operas and oratorios, of which *Messiah* is best known.

The Classical period

Methods of musical composition continued to develop throughout the eighteenth century, and the years from about 1750 to 1800 are known as the Classical period. We call this the Classical period because at that time people looked back for inspiration to the days of ancient Greece and Rome. This Classical influence is reflected in their painting and architecture, and similarly, we can compare the music of the period with a Greek temple, in which every column and angle adds up to a perfectly proportioned building.

Above *Wolfgang Amadeus Mozart (1756–91) as a small boy, with his sister and his father Leopold. He was a child prodigy, who began composing when he was five years old, though nearly all his greatest music was written during the last six years of his life.*

"Sonata form" was a new way of constructing a single piece of music with well-balanced contrasts of theme and mood. There were also symphonies and concertos for the orchestra, and sonatas and string quartets for solo instruments or smaller instrumental groups. Much of this was called chamber music, that is, music for performance at home rather than in a larger palace or public place. Such works consisted of three or four individual pieces or movements that contrasted well with each other in terms of tempo (speed of rhythm) and mood.

This period was also the time when the orchestra, as we know it, came into being. In their symphonies and concertos, composers wished their music to sound well-balanced, with each instrument or group of instruments playing the parts of the music that suited them best: hence the organization of the orchestra into its "families" of strings, woodwind, brass, and percussion.

The two great composers of the Classical period were Franz Joseph Haydn and Mozart. Haydn built up the forms of the symphony and string quartet from their beginnings. Mozart, who composed some of the finest operas, added the same expressive beauty to his symphonies, concertos, and other instrumental works. Beethoven developed the Classical principles of Haydn and Mozart in his symphonies, concertos, sonatas, and string quartets. But Beethoven lived right at the end of the Classical period, at the time of the French Revolution and Napoleonic Wars. His *Eroica* Symphony was inspired by Napoleon. His music has the same revolutionary force and power; and it largely opened the way for the next musical period, which is known as the Romantic period.

Romantic music

Most composers before Beethoven had been employed by the Church or the aristocracy. Most composers after him struck out on their own, believing they had the right to use their art to express their personal ideas and feelings. That was the spirit of the Romantic movement of the nineteenth century, when music took many forms. Schubert wrote symphonies, sonatas, and string quartets; but he also created what was virtually a new musical form with his hundreds of dramatic and expressive songs (*Lieder* as they are called in German). Schumann, Chopin, and Liszt wrote expressive piano pieces. Berlioz had a marvelous feeling for the instruments of the orchestra, blending sounds much like a painter mixing colors on his palette, to create vivid musical "pictures." In Russia, Tchaikovsky, Rimsky-Korsakov, and others wrote just as brilliantly and vividly for a large orchestra.

Some Romantic composers were much influenced by the political and revolutionary upheavals of the time, and wrote patriotic or "nationalistic" music. Chopin composed "polonaises" in honor of his Polish homeland, while Smetana and Dvořák incorporated the folk music of their native Bohemia into many of their compositions. This nationalist feeling was shared by other composers; by

Below *Robert Schumann (1810–56) and his wife Clara (1819–1896) were two of the most important figures in Romantic music. After Robert's death, Clara pursued her own career as a pianist. She was a close and valued friend of the composer Johannes Brahams (1833–97).*

Below *Conducting, as we know it, dates from about the time of Beethoven, when orchestras grew larger and composers began writing more complex music for them. Here Sir George Solti, one of today's top conductors, is rehearsing with the London Philharmonic Orchestra, and instructing the musicians how he wants the music played.*

Mussorgsky in Russia, Grieg in Norway, Sibelius in Finland, de Falla in Spain, Elgar in England. They all, in a sense, flew a musical flag for their countries.

Not all composers of the time were so "Romantic" in the ways just described. Brahms put together the ideas we consider Classical with those that we consider Romantic. He composed symphonies, concertos, and chamber music that stayed close to Classical forms, and he also wrote lyrical and expressive *Lieder* and piano pieces.

Above *Bulgarian folk dancers at the turn of the century. The Hungarian composer Béla Bartók (1881–1945) made a study of the folk songs and dances of Eastern Europe, and these had a strong influence on his music. Many other composers have also been inspired by folk music.*

Right *Claude Monet, created this impressionist painting using his paint brush. The French composers Claude Debussy (1862–1918) and Maurice Ravel (1875–1937) created the same moods or "impressions" of sky, water, and trees in some of their music, achieving their impressionist effect with strange and beautiful new harmonies.*

Mendelssohn too, combined Classical and Romantic ideas, composing symphonies and string quartets in the Classical style and also some wonderfully descriptive music.

Mendelssohn was also one of the first great conductors. Early instrumental music was performed in strict tempo, but the complexity of new works required more variety to give depth and expression to the music. Conductors now became a familiar part of the musical scene, allowing musicians to perform together with more understanding.

Music of our century

At the start of the twentieth century, two leading composers, Gustav Mahler and Richard Strauss, wrote large and complex symphonies or symphonic poems with "programs" – music conveying particular moods and feelings, or describing scenes and events. Other composers began to think that this was as far as Romantic music could go, and that they must create new musical styles and forms.

Claude Debussy and Maurice Ravel created original and subtle new harmonies, inspired to some extent by the work of the French impressionist painters. Many of Bartók's compositions were inspired by the strong, sometimes wild melodies and rhythms of Hungarian and Rumanian folk music. Igor Stravinsky shook the musical world with the orchestral sounds and rhythms he created in his ballet *The Rite of Spring*. Arnold Schoenberg invented an entirely new kind of scale, called the dodecaphonic, or twelve-tone scale. This was like a new alphabet, and most people found his new musical "language" very difficult to understand. More recently, Boulez has combined some of Schoenberg's ideas with the kind of electronic sounds we have discussed on pages 15 and 16.

However, not all of this century's composers have written such "advanced" music. Sergei Rachmaninov's symphonies and concertos sound rich and romantic. Aaron Copland in the United States and Sergei Prokofiev in the Soviet Union wrote music with a popular appeal. Another Soviet composer, Dmitri Shostakovich, captured the heroism and horror following Hitler's invasion of Russia during World War II in some of his powerful symphonies.

One other notable development has been some composers' interest in oriental music and ideas. Olivier Messiaen's *Turangalila* Symphony is inspired by images of Hindu gods. One of Karlheinz Stockhausen's most interesting works, for two electronically aided pianos, wood blocks, and bells, is titled *Mantra*, the Indian word for a method of religious and mystical meditation.

Below *The size of orchestras can vary, from about thirty-five players to over a hundred. But the plan of an orchestra remains much the same, no matter how many players there are. The strings, the largest section, are mainly at the front. Behind them are the woodwind, brass, and percussion sections. If a choir is needed, it is usually arranged behind the orchestra, or placed on either side of it.*

5 Opera

Some of the most familiar and best-loved music comes from operas. People everywhere know the "Toreador's Song" from Georges Bizet's *Carmen*, and Richard Wagner's exciting "Ride of the Valkyries." Opera – sung drama – is the most exciting kind of entertainment. It has made the fortunes of some composers and singers, and it has broken the hearts of others who have failed. There are no half-measures in the glittering world of opera.

Italian opera

The Italian people have a special love of singing; so it is no surprise that opera began in their country. It was, to start with, a scholarly attempt to revive ancient Greek drama, which was known to include a kind of chanting. But Claudio Monteverdi, who lived at the end of the Renaissance, wrote operas with dramatic stories and songs (arias), including instrumental music to accompany the singers.

Below Aida *is a spectacular opera by Verdi. It is a dramatic story set in the days of ancient Egypt. Verdi was asked to compose it as part of the celebrations for the opening of the Suez Canal in 1869, though it was not finished in time.*

The ingredients of opera were soon established. A poet would write a libretto, which was the text of a drama for a composer to set to music. This mostly took the form of "recitative" – a way of exchanging dialogue in a singsong voice – and arias, sung by one or other of the characters. The singers were the stars of opera, often earning far more money than the composer or librettist.

In the eighteenth century, the main kind of opera was *opera seria*, or serious opera of the kind that Handel wrote. The libretto was usually based on stories from Greek mythology or ancient history. But audiences didn't take such operas too seriously. They cheered their favorite singers, booed the ones they didn't like, ate and drank throughout performances, and generally had a good time. There was also *opera buffa*, or comic opera, often about an old man chasing after a pretty girl and making a fool of himself.

In the Romantic period of the nineteenth century, Italian opera composers such as Rossini, Bellini, and Donizetti wrote arias that gave singers a chance to demonstrate their vocal power and skills. Verdi composed more dramatic operas, portraying such characters as Rigoletto, the hunchbacked court jester who has his own daughter murdered by mistake. Verdi was a hero to the Italian people, because they identified the stirring music of his operas with their desire, which he supported, for national independence and unity. Puccini, too, picked exciting plots for his operas, and moved audiences to tears with his soaring melodies and lively use of the orchestra.

French and German opera

Returning to the seventeenth century, there had been a specially grand kind of opéra-ballet performed in France. It began at the court of Louis XIV and was intended, like his Palace of Versailles, to add to the splendor of his reign. Opéra-ballet, of course, contained dancing as well as singing, and for a long time to come, nearly all operas in France included a ballet sequence.

The German-born composer Christoph Gluck admired the grandeur of French opéra-ballet, and also wanted to reform all opera so that music and drama were more closely related. Mozart, in Vienna, learned from Gluck. By the beauty of his own music, Mozart brought comedy and drama together in two of his finest Italian-style operas, *The Marriage of Figaro* and *Don Giovanni*. By contrast, Mozart's *The Magic Flute* is a kind of pantomime (*Singspiel*) in which the singers speak their lines of dialogue, as in an ordinary play. After Mozart, Beethoven and Carl Maria von Weber also wrote German operas with spoken dialogue.

The German composer Wagner united music, poetry, and spectacle into "music-drama" – to him the highest form of art. His mature operas are like great tapestries of sound, in which orchestra and singers blend as one. Wagner's most ambitious work was *The Ring of the Nibelungs*, a music-drama in four parts. Based on ancient myths and legends, it tells of a golden ring with a terrible curse upon it, and how it brings death and destruction to the world.

Above *Richard Wagner (1813–83) was a controversial figure both in his music and his politics. His operas were more visionary and complex than any before or since.*

Below *A scene from Wagner's opera* The Mastersingers of Nuremberg, *which recalled the festivals of poetry and song held in Nuremberg during the Renaissance.*

Right *The Spanish tenor Placido Domingo (1941–) in the role of Radames in* Aida. *Besides needing beautiful, powerful voices, opera stars have to sing very difficult music and to act their roles with conviction.*

Inset *A scene from* Don Giovanni, *by Mozart. Here the stone statue of a man killed by the wicked Don comes to life and drags his murderer down to hell. No one before Mozart had written such dramatic music for an opera.*

Opera today

Wagner would never have been able to stage *The Ring of the Nibelungs* without money from King Ludwig II of Bavaria. With the King's help, he even built his own opera house in the Bavarian town of Bayreuth. Today, there are no monarchs like King Ludwig, to shower money on opera composers; and some people say that opera is too costly to last much longer. Obviously it is very expensive to produce. There are the costs of orchestra and singers (usually with a large chorus as well as soloists); stage and costume designs; a stage director and a musical conductor; and all the backstage workers. But opera survives, because people love the music, the glamour, and the excitement of it.

Today, many opera companies are subsidized by governments, or are sponsored by commercial companies. And though it is such a risky business, composers still write operas. This century one of the most successful of them has been Benjamin Britten. Two of his operas are *Peter Grimes*, the tragic story of a fisherman, and *Let's Make an Opera!*, with parts mainly for children, and a part for the audience also.

Below *Opera is an important form of music in China. Oriental opera differs from opera in the West in that it follows a rigid set of rules, not necessarily drawn from life. The actions and emotions of the performers are often portrayed in the singing of simple songs accompanied by instrumental music.*

Some Famous Operas

Mozart	*Don Giovanni*
	The Magic Flute
Beethoven	*Fidelio*
Rossini	*The Barber of Seville*
Verdi	*Rigoletto*
	Aida
Bizet	*Carmen*
Wagner	*Tannhäuser*
Puccini	*La Bohème*
	Madame Butterfly
Gershwin	*Porgy and Bess*
Britten	*Peter Grimes*
	Billy Budd

⑥ From Popular to Pop

There has always been popular music – that is, music enjoyed by large numbers of people. The symphonies of Beethoven and the operas of Verdi are popular pieces of music, if we think of the millions who have loved listening to them. But the starting point for what we generally think of as popular music is the nineteenth century. It was then that large numbers of people in the new industrial cities of Europe and America started demanding the kind of music they liked best.

Back in the eighteenth century, in London, people had enjoyed a very popular theatrical show called *The Beggar's Opera*, which used the tunes of songs and dances that everybody knew and liked. Toward the end of the nineteenth century, some of the most popular music of the time was also performed in theaters. There were variety shows, known as music hall in Britain and vaudeville in the United States, where entertainers presented a series of acts. Many entertainers were singers, whose songs were lighthearted or sentimental expressions of the hard life of working-class people, or they were funny and "suggestive." Like many vocalists in popular music, their stage personalities and their style of song were far more important than the actual quality of their voices.

Above *Scott Joplin (1868–1917) composed piano pieces called ragtime, a style of music that helped to popularize jazz in the early years of this century.*

Below *A scene from* West Side Story, *a stage and film musical based on Shakespeare's play* Romeo and Juliet. *It is set in New York City, to music written by the American composer and conductor Leonard Bernstein (1918–).*

Operetta was more sophisticated, but was very lighthearted, sentimental, and sometimes satirical, with tuneful melodies. Johann Strauss and Franz Lehár in Vienna, Jacques Offenbach in Paris, and the partnership of Gilbert and Sullivan in London, were all very successful creators of operettas.

The nineteenth century also saw dancing organized on a mass scale as popular recreation. The old courtly dances and folk dances of earlier times gave way to the waltz and the polka, in the new gas-lit ballrooms of the age, or in public parks. Indeed, the Viennese waltzes of Johann Strauss and others were probably the most truly popular music there has ever been. They were also considered sinful by some, because gentlemen put their arm around the ladies' waists!

The operettas and dances of the nineteenth century were as popular in the United States as in Europe, and led to the even more successful stage and film musicals of this century – most of them American – by such famous songwriters and composers as Irving Berlin, George and Ira Gershwin, Jerome Kern, Cole Porter, Richard Rodgers and Oscar Hammerstein II, Stephen Sondheim, Leonard Bernstein, Andrew Lloyd Webber, and many others.

Popular music in the United States in the early twentieth century was much the same as in Europe, because most Americans were Europeans by descent. But there were also Americans of a quite different ancestry; black people whose ancestors, as we have read on page 21, had been brought from Africa as slaves; and others who were half black and half French or Spanish, or partly American Indian. From this vigorous mixture of cultures came the music of jazz.

Above *The waltz was the most popular dance of the nineteenth century, largely thanks to the beautiful melodies of the Viennese composer Johann Strauss II (1825–99). These include the famous* Blue Danube *and* Emperor Waltz *– music that is still very popular today.*

Left *The jazz trumpeter and singer Louis Armstrong (1900–1971) was a brilliant improviser, making up music on the spur of the moment. He was also a great personality, nicknamed "Satchmo."*

Below *The songwriter and composer George Gershwin (1899–1937). Among his best-known works are the orchestral pieces* Rhapsody in Blue, Concerto in F, An American in Paris, *and the opera* Porgy and Bess. *He also wrote music for many stage and film musicals.*

Jazz began in and around the seaport of New Orleans, in the early years of this century. There were sad songs, called "blues," lamenting the hard, often cruel life of the black men and women who worked on the old cotton plantations of the southern states; but also livelier pieces, owing something in style to the military marches of the Civil War (1861–65), called rags and stomps.

Few of these early jazz musicians could read music, so improvisation was an important element of their performances. Much of the music sounded rough-and-ready, compared with the more genteel European songs and dances; but it had certain harmonies and syncopated, off-beat rhythms, that were new and catchy. As black people moved to St. Louis, Chicago, and other big cities in search of work, jazz became more widely appreciated. At the same time, the invention of phonograph recording meant that people everywhere could hear the music of Ferdinand "Jelly Roll" Morton and his band of Red Hot Peppers, of trumpeter Louis Armstrong, and other jazz pioneers. By 1930, jazz had entered the mainstream of popular entertainment throughout the Western world.

Some composers were delighted by it too. Debussy and Ravel in France, and Copland in the United States, all used elements of jazz in some of their compositions. Gershwin regarded jazz as the true sound of American music, and he wanted it taken seriously in his *Rhapsody in Blue* and other jazz-style concert works, and in his all-black opera *Porgy and Bess.*

The main influence of jazz, however, continued to be on music with
mass appeal. There were jazzy dances, such as the Charleston, and
others with a blend of Latin American rhythms, that became almost
as popular around the world as the waltz had been in the nineteenth
century. The huge popularity of jazz-style dance music attracted
many musicians to play in dance bands. Simultaneously, the
invention and commercial development of radio followed that of the
phonograph, and band leaders wanted to reach the widest possible
audience. They softened and sweetened the sounds of jazz, even
adding such instruments as violins. The result was "swing," the
popular music of the 1930s and 1940s. It was heard everywhere; on
radio, on film, and in the big public dance halls, where millions went
to enjoy themselves on Saturday nights. The old jazz bands had
singers with powerful voices, like Bessie Smith, who were used to
singing in noisy bars and cafés, or in the open air. The swing bands
had vocalists too, but they would almost whisper or "croon" their
songs into a microphone. Bing Crosby and Frank Sinatra, two very
famous entertainers, began their careers as crooners.

In the early days of jazz, a black pianist, Clarence "Pinetop" Smith,
played what can be described as a speeded-up version of the blues,
called "boogie." He was killed in a gangland fight (a reminder of the
rough, sometimes dangerous life of many jazz musicians), so he
never lived to see, in the 1950s, how boogie suddenly changed into

rock 'n' roll (taking its name from the new, liberated style of dancing that went along with it), to start the greatest revolution of all in the world of popular music.

Bill Haley and the Comets, Elvis Presley, and Chuck Berry, in the United States, were the superstars of rock 'n' roll. In the 1960s, The Beatles in England introduced a new sound to rock 'n' roll with their "Liverpool" or "Mersey" sound. All these stars performed in small groups, their principal instruments being electric guitars and drums. The big swing bands had almost disappeared. But there was more change to come. For the first time, young people, teenage girls and boys, with money to spend, influenced popular musical tastes. A large part of the entertainment industry was geared to meet their demands. Popular music became "Pop."

Pop music has exploded into a bewildering variety of styles. Rhythm and blues, soul, and other styles have remained fairly close to existing jazz and other types of popular music. Such groups as The Rolling Stones and Led Zeppelin pioneered hard rock and heavy metal. As these titles suggest, they are tougher, more strident

Below *Bill Haley and the Comets, pioneers of rock 'n' roll in the 1950s. Their recording of* Rock Around the Clock *was a sensational hit.*

musical styles. Punk rock was even more strident and anarchic, reflecting the sense of alienation and anger felt by many young people growing up in a hard commercial world threatened also by nuclear war. By way of contrast, there has been the psychedelic music of groups such as Pink Floyd and The Doors. They created strange, dream-like, electronically aided sound effects, associated with hallucinatory drugs.

Pop music has influenced the life-style, or culture, of whole generations. It has expressed changing social and moral attitudes toward such aspects of modern life as drug-taking (which has claimed the lives of several stars, including guitarist Jimi Hendrix, singer Janis Joplin, and British punk rocker Sid Vicious). Pop music has also inspired several socially acceptable hit musicals, *Jesus Christ Superstar* and *Godspell*. Reggae, calypso, and other forms, originating in the Caribbean, have their own links with religion and politics. Above all, pop music has crossed racial, social, and political barriers around the world with such performers as Michael Jackson.

The singer Tina Turner (1938–) is a very successful pop artist. She has managed to keep pace with the ever-changing tastes and styles in pop music – a tremendous challenge for such stars.

7 Recording and Broadcasting

Until the beginning of this century, and the invention of the phonograph, the only way to hear music was "live." Visits to concerts were rare and precious occasions; and people often played instruments or sang in their homes, to entertain each other. Today, many musicians spend far more time, and earn far more money, recording or broadcasting, than playing in live concerts.

This transformation of the musical scene began with the phonograph, which was invented by two Americans, Thomas Edison and Alexander Graham Bell. They recorded sound vibrations as grooves of varying depth on a waxed cylinder. When the cylinder was revolved, these vibrations were picked up by a needle and reproduced, through a loudspeaker, as sound. But only after discs had replaced cylinders, and other refinements had been introduced, in the early years of this century, did the recording industry really begin to grow.

In those early days of "acoustic" recording, the artists had to sing or play as close as possible into a type of large trumpet or horn. The most famous recording stars were singers with strong voices; Enrico Caruso and Nellie Melba from the world of opera, and jazz vocalists Ma Rainey and Bessie Smith. But in the 1920s, acoustic was replaced by electric recording, in which sounds were picked up by a microphone.

Below *The music of a dance band being recorded in a modern recording studio.*

Inset *The Australian singer Dame Nellie Melba (1861–1931) making a gramophone recording. Early recording stars needed strong voices – they sang directly into the recording apparatus. Later, sounds were picked up by microphones.*

The quality of recording was much improved, and it was also possible to make more copies or pressings of a recording. Recorded music of all kinds – opera, symphonic music, jazz, and dance-music was big business. At about the same time, sound was added to vision in the movies, giving another impetus to recorded music; and such composers as Prokofiev and William Walton wrote some fine music especially for films, as others had written incidental music for stage plays.

Caruso and Ma Rainey would be lost in a modern recording studio. Microphones strategically placed around the musicians are linked to a multi-track tape recorder, which registers their signals as electromagnetic impulses. These are combined on a master tape or disc. Recorded "takes" can be played back, and errors corrected by a "retake" of a particular passage, which is then incorporated into the finished recording. The latest advance is digital recording, whereby the signals from the microphones are processed by a computer into millions of coded digits (numbers). Compact discs carry this code, which is interpreted and converted back to sound, with the aid of a laser beam. Technicians as well as musicians are responsible for the success of a modern recording.

Today we can buy analog (electrically-copied) phonograph records; digital compact discs; analog or digital casette tapes for use in the home or for stereos in cars. And there is an endless stream of new recordings, of every conceivable type of music. All this in addition to radio and television. We can have music around the clock, every moment of our lives. But we must not take it all for granted; if we dull our senses with too much, then our ability to listen intelligently is soon diminished.

A disc jockey at work in a broadcasting studio. His choice of records could make or break the career of a pop musician or group.

Where to Hear and See "Live" Music

Music is the most popular and widely practiced of all the arts. There are many opportunities to learn music, either at school or with a private teacher. Most high schools have a good music department with facilities to learn both traditional and electronic instruments. You may be able to join a choir, band, or orchestra at school, or within the local community. Private classes teaching a variety of instruments, and singing lessons, are advertised in local newspapers and are listed in the classified section of the telephone directory.

If you are thinking of taking up music professionally, you should ask your music teacher for advice. For those hoping for a career as an instrumentalist or singer in an orchestra, band, opera, or other stage, film, or television presentation, there are music colleges and schools throughout the country, providing courses for students in most branches of music. The time to start thinking about entering a music college is while you are still at school.

The best way to enter the pop music scene is probably to get to know members of a local group, and by reading music journals that carry classified advertisements for pop musicians and singers. Remember that the world of pop music is strictly commercial and there are no academic or other institutions. You will need to persevere to make your own way in the pop "jungle."

School guidance counselors, libraries and other information centers will be able to give advice on a career in many branches of music. Although progress is better mapped out for students in the world of traditional music, the competition is just as intense as it is in the pop world and standards are high.

Good luck!

Getting Involved in Music

In almost any sizeable community in the United States or Canada you will have many opportunities to see and hear a great variety of musical performances.

Most major cities, such as Chicago, Los Angeles, Pittsburgh, Philadelphia, New York, Boston, San Francisco, Houston, Cincinnati, Cleveland, Toronto, Montreal, and Vancouver have world renowned symphony orchestras that play classical music. These orchestras go on tour periodically. In addition, many cities including New York, Chicago, and San Francisco have fine opera companies which attract principal singers from all over the world and maintain regular schedules of performances.

Music festivals are held usually during the summer in various vacation spots, such as Tanglewood in Massachusetts, or Waterloo Village in New Jersey. If you want to hear "mostly Mozart," there is an annual festival of that name in New York's Lincoln Center. In addition, there is a Mozart festival in Salzburg, Austria, birthplace of the composer; Wagner festivals are held at Bayreuth, West Germany, where Wagner's opera house was built. Famous festivals are also held in Aix-en-Provence, France, and Spoleto, Italy, each year. The Spoleto Festival has branched out with an American counterpart held in Charleston, S.C., during the summer.

Orchestras at music festivals are composed not only of professionals, but also of young performers who may be joining an orchestra for the first time. In addition, there are music camps throughout North America that cater to young hopefuls. For information about these camps you should contact your school guidance counselor or music teacher who undoubtedly has information or can tell you where to acquire it.

In addition, some North American cities are noted for special kinds of music. In New Orleans you can still hear and see Dixieland jazz bands perform. In Boston, there's the Pops Orchestra, which performs more popular classical music and show tunes in an informal atmosphere. In Miami and the cities of the Southwest you can hear Latin music. And in Nashville, Tennessee, there's the home of country and western music, the Grand Old Opry. Probably the most popular means of seeing performances of pop music is via television. In addition, live jazz and pop music can be heard in concerts at major sports arenas, as well as at jazz and rock festivals.

For details about all these performances look in your local newspaper or contact the local concert hall for information.

Glossary

Blues A classic jazz form, twelve bars long, which includes particular harmonies.

Cantata A composition for voices, usually with instruments.

Chord The sounding together of two or more notes of different pitch; the most usual form of harmony.

Concerto Italian word, meaning "together." The concerto grosso (great concerto), usually consisted of two groups of stringed instruments.

Counterpoint Ways of combining melodies to create a kind of musical pattern. The adjective is **contrapuntal**.

Fugue A type of contrapuntal piece in which the notes of a musical theme are interwoven.

Incidental music Traditionally, music to accompany a stage play; but film and television music is of a similar kind.

Key In harmony, the name or title of each of the twelve major and minor scales. Also the name for the levers on a keyboard instrument.

Keyboard The row of keys which the player presses to sound the notes.

Mass A choral composition, setting to music the words of the principal service of the Roman Catholic Church. A Requiem Mass is sung in memory of the dead.

Modes The scales on which medieval church music was based.

Movement A single piece of music, usually making up part of a larger work.

Note A musical sound of definite fundamental frequency or pitch. Also, any of a series of written signs representing a musical sound.

Octave A span of eight pitched notes in any major or minor scale.

Opera A combination of music and drama. **Operetta** means "little opera," or light opera.

Oratorio A dramatic (unstaged) musical composition based on a religious theme, usually requiring a choir, soloists, and instruments.

Overture A piece of orchestral music played at the beginning of an opera, ballet, or other stage work; or a fairly short piece of concert music.

Plainsong Unaccompanied vocal music sung in some church services.

Polonaise French name for a stately Polish dance, with three beats to the bar.

Polyphonic music Music played or sung in several melodic lines or parts.

Rhapsody A piece of music in a fairly free form, popular with Romantic composers.

Scale A group of pitched notes taken in ascending or descending order; especially within one octave: a chromatic scale includes all the notes on a piano keyboard; a pentatonic scale is a five-note scale.

Sonata Most usually, a composition for piano, or piano and one other instrument, in three or four movements.

Spiritual A type of religious song originating among black slaves in the South.

Symphony Most usually, a large-scale orchestral composition in four movements. Some symphonies include singing.

Tempo The speed or pace of a piece of music, as distinct from its basic rhythm.

Virginals A type of small harpsichord.

Further Reading

Music by DAVID MOSES (Kingfisher, 1986)

Music, An Illustrated Encyclopedia by NEIL ARDLEY (Hamlyn, 1986)

Music and Musicians by EVA BAILEY (Batsford, 1983)

New Encyclopedia of Music by ALAN BLACKWOOD (Ward Lock, 1983)

The Oxford Junior Companion to Music by MICHAEL HURD (Oxford University Press, 1979)

The Performing World of the Musician by CHRISTOPHER HEADINGTON (Hamish Hamilton, 1981)

Twenty Names in Classical Music by ALAN BLACKWOOD (Wayland, 1987)

Twenty Names in Pop Music by ANDREW LANGLEY (Wayland, 1987)

The Voice of Music by ROBINA BECKLE WILLSON (Heinemann, 1976)

Index

Picture Acknowledgments

Aquarius 7, 29, 32–3, 35 (lower), 37 (top), 38 (top), 39, 40; BBC Hulton 25, 37 (top); Bridgeman Art Library 24, 30 (lower); J. Allan Cash 18, 21; Chapel Studios 8; David Cumming 10; Donald Cooper 34 (lower); Mary Evans 5 (lower), 26 upper and lower, 27, 28, 30 (top), 33, 34 (top), 38 (lower), 43 (top); Michael Holford 4; Camilla Jessell 14; Marion and Tony Morrison 5 (top), 19, 20 (inset); David Redfern 15 (top), 41; Sussex Publications 17; Topham Picture Library 15 (lower), 16, 35 (right), 42; Wayland Picture Library 13, 23, 36, 43 (lower), 44; Zefa 6, 9, 19 (inset), 20, 22. Artwork on pages 9, 10, 12, 31 by Malcolm Walker.